Tyrannosaurus Rex

BY BARBARA ALPERT

amicus
high interest

Amicus High Interest is published by Amicus
P.O. Box 1329, Mankato, MN 56002
www.amicuspublishing.us

Library of Congress Cataloging-in-Publication Data
Alpert, Barbara.
 Tyrannosaurus rex / by Barbara Alpert.
    p. cm. -- (Digging for dinosaurs)
 Summary: "Describes how the Tyrannosaurus Rex was
discovered, how paleontologists study its bones, and what the
fossil evidence tells us about the behavior of the largest meat-
eating dinosaur"-- Provided by publisher.
 Audience: K to grade 3.
 Includes bibliographical references and index.
 ISBN 978-1-60753-369-6 (library binding) -- ISBN 978-1-
60753-417-4 (ebook)
1. Tyrannosaurus rex--Juvenile literature. I. Title.
 QE862.S3A4354 2014
 567.912--dc23

                              2013001230

Editor   Rebecca Glaser
Series Designer   Kathleen Petelinsek
Page production   Red Line Editorial, Inc.

Photo Credits
Shutterstock Images, cover, 25; Stocktrek Images/SuperStock,
4, 7; Roland T. Bird/Getty Images, 9; AP Images, 10; William
Diller Matthew, 13; Francois Gohier/Science Source, 14;
Micha Fleuren/Shutterstock Images, 16; Tom Williams/
Getty Images, 19; Mark A. Schneider/Science Source, 21;
SuperStock, 22; Yakobchuk Vasyl/Shutterstock Images, 26;
Richard T. Nowitz/Science Source, 29

Printed in the United States of America at Corporate Graphics
in North Mankato, Minnesota.
5-2013 / P.O. 1148
10 9 8 7 6 5 4 3 2 1

Table of Contents

Tyrannosaurus rex kills a
Triceratops for its next meal.

Q How do we know that T. rex ate Triceratops?

King of the Dinosaurs

Tyrannosaurus rex turned its huge head. Its nostrils opened wide. Something nearby smelled good to eat. The dinosaur lifted its head above the trees. There! A young Triceratops munched on a plant. There was no escape! T. rex opened its jaws and bit its **prey**. The Triceratops fought back with its horns. But T. rex was too strong.

From **fossils**. Some Triceratops bones show T. rex bite marks.

Tyrannosaurus rex was one of the biggest meat-eaters. It was as long as a school bus. But it was twice as tall! It had long, sharp teeth. If a few teeth broke, new ones grew. Scientists have studied T. rex's jaws. They think it ate up to 500 pounds (225 kg) in one bite!

T. Rex had strong jaws and sharp teeth for eating meat.

The Discovery of Tyrannosaurus Rex

It was 1902. A **paleontologist** named Barnum Brown was in Montana. He found huge dinosaur bones. It took a few years—and some **dynamite**—to get them out. The fossils were stuck in huge chunks of rock. Horses pulled them to a train station. Then the fossils were sent to New York.

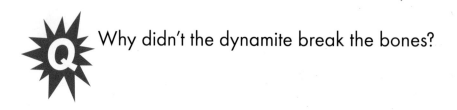 Why didn't the dynamite break the bones?

Brown dug up fossils in Montana and at this site in Texas.

 Brown's crew put the dynamite in just the right spots. It cracked the cliff. Then they used tools to pull apart big pieces.

Henry Osborn named Tyrannosaurus rex in 1905.

 Q What does Tyrannosaurus rex mean?

Henry Osborn was Brown's boss. He worked at the American Museum of Natural History in New York. Workers there used drills and hammers. They got the bones out of the rock. Osborn studied them. In 1905, he named the new dinosaur Tyrannosaurus rex. He later looked at bones Brown found in 1900. They were from a T. rex too!

It means "king of the **tyrant** lizards." T. rex was the biggest meat-eating dinosaur anyone had found.

Brown kept looking for bones. One day he spotted a giant skull in a wall of rock. It was whole. And it was 4 feet (1.2 m) long! Other parts of the T. rex **skeleton** were buried nearby. It was put on display. This was the most complete T. rex found for 80 years.

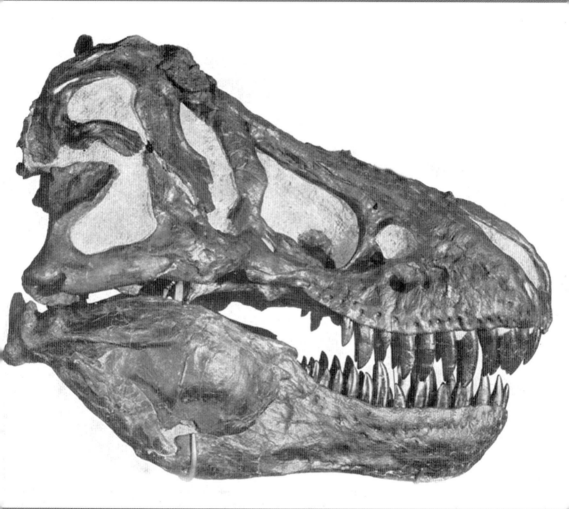

More T. Rex Fossils!

Harley Garbani was a plumber. But he loved to hunt for fossils. In 1966, the Los Angeles County Museum sent him to Montana. There he saw some huge foot bones. He knew they were from a T. rex. His crew dug up more of the skeleton. The skull was almost 5 feet (1.5 m) long!

This T. rex pelvis (hip bone) was found in South Dakota.

Dinosaur bones can be buried
in dirt or hidden in rock.

Q Could you find dinosaur bones?

In 1980, Jeff Baker was in high school. He lived in Alberta, Canada. While on a fishing trip, he went for a walk. He spotted large dinosaur bones by a river. They were black. A local museum sent a crew to dig them up. They were from a Tyrannosaurus rex. Minerals in the soil had turned them black.

 Yes, if you live where dinosaurs lived. All you need are good eyes. Fossil hunters look for what is strange or different.

Sue Hendrickson is a fossil hunter. In 1990, she was in South Dakota. She saw three large backbones, or **vertebrae**, and a leg bone. They were sticking out of a cliff. Their shape told her: meat-eater. Their size said: had to be T. rex! The bones were dug out. Almost the whole skeleton was there! The dinosaur was named Sue.

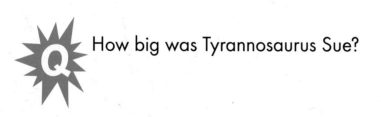 How big was Tyrannosaurus Sue?

Tourists crowd around Sue the T. rex at a museum in Chicago.

A It was 42 feet (13 m) long. At the time, it was the biggest T. rex ever found.

Fossil Clues to Study

When Osborn first named Tyrannosaurus rex, he wondered about its short arms. They were too short to reach its mouth. Its claws were strong. What were they for? Some scientists think its arms held prey to eat it. Others guess T. rex used claws for fighting. No one knows for sure.

This T. rex claw is 3.5 inches (9 cm) long. It was found in South Dakota.

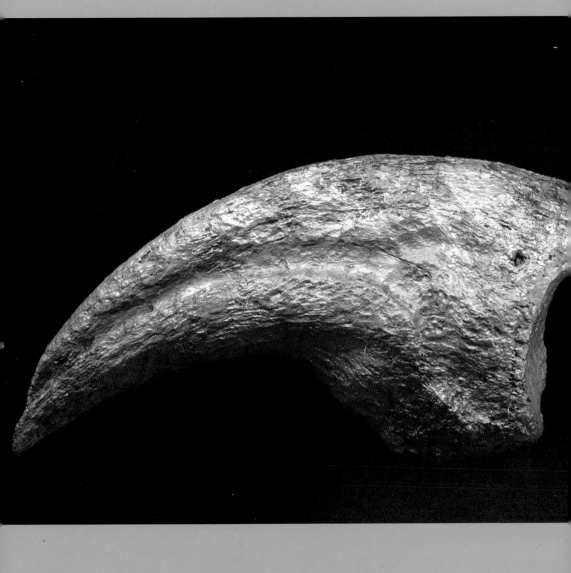

Dinosaur tracks show how these big animals walked.

Q What do dinosaur footprints tell us?

T. rex tracks are very hard to find. In 1983, a man was hiking in New Mexico. He saw a huge footprint. It had three toes, like a T. rex. But there were no T. rex bones nearby. In 2007, a large footprint was found in Montana. It was found near T. rex fossils. It could be from a Tyrannosaurus rex.

 They show a dinosaur's foot shape. Deep prints show how heavy it was. They can show how fast it moved and how it stood up.

Most T. rex fossils are found alone. In 2000, a crew was digging in Montana. They found five T. rexes. They were all in the same area. One was bigger than Sue!

The Tarbosaurus is a close relative of T. rex. In China, many Tarbosauruses have been found together. Some scientists think this means they hunted in packs.

Do you think T. rex lived alone or in groups?

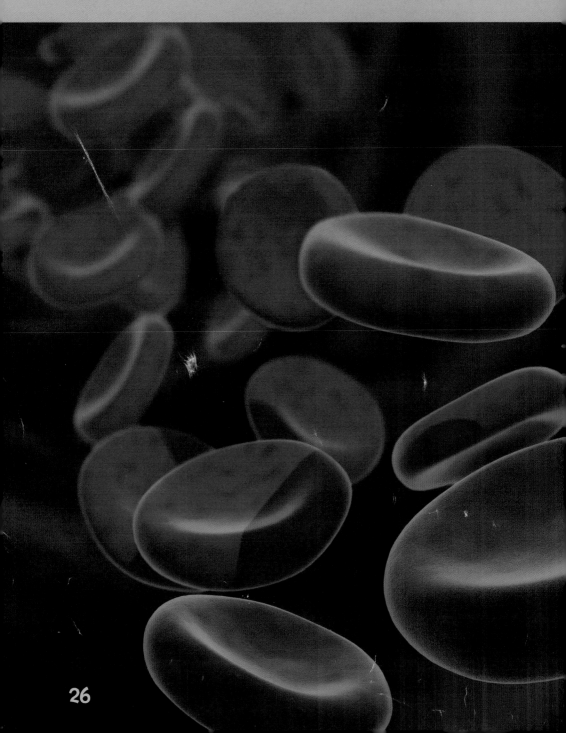

Dr. Schweitzer found a way to study T. rex blood cells.

Tyrannosaurus Rex Today

Modern science helps us study fossils. In 2005, Dr. Mary Schweitzer tried something new. She put a broken T. rex leg bone in acid. The acid dissolved the bone. But soft **tissue** was left. She looked at it under a microscope. She saw red blood cells and blood vessels! It was the first time anyone found soft tissue from a dinosaur.

Tyrannosaurus rex fossils have only been found in North America. But in 2009, scientists found a fossil in China. It looked just like T. rex. It had the same big head and sharp teeth. It had tiny arms. But it was much smaller. And it lived 60 million years earlier. Scientists think it was an ancestor of T. rex. They named it Raptorex.

Scientists keep looking for fossil clues about dinosaurs.

Glossary

dynamite An explosive used to break up rocks.

fossil The remains of a plant or animal of a past age preserved in earth or rock.

paleontologist A scientist who studies fossils.

prey Animals that other animals eat.

skeleton The frame of bones supporting a body.

tissue A group of cells in an animal's body.

tyrant A mean ruler who has all the power.

vertebrae Bones in an animal's back.

Read More

Bailey, Gerry. *Tyrannosaurus rex*. Smithsonian Prehistoric Zone. New York: Crabtree Publishing Company, 2011.

Parker, Steve. *100 Things You Should Know About T. rex*. Broomall, Penn: Mason Crest Publishers, 2011.

Riggs, Kate. *Tyrannosaurus Rex*. When Dinosaurs Lived. Mankato, MN: Creative Paperbacks, 2012.

Websites

T-rex: Enchanted Learning
http://www.enchantedlearning.com/subjects/dinosaurs/dinos/trex/index.shtml

The T-rex | thedinsosaurs.org | Everything Kids Need to Know about Dinosaurs!
http://www.thedinosaurs.org/dinosaurs/trex.aspx

Tyrannosaurus Facts and Pictures—National Geographic Kids
http://kids.nationalgeographic.com/kids/animals/creaturefeature/tyrannosaurus-rex/

Index

About the Author

Barbara Alpert has written more than 20 children's books and many books for adults. She lives in New York City, where she works as an editor. She loves to travel and has collected fossils in New York, New Jersey, Montana, and Pennsylvania.